SCHIRMER'S LIBRARY
OF MUSICAL CLASSICS

Compositions for the Piano
FRÉDÉRIC CHOPIN

Edited, Revised, and Fingered by
RAFAEL JOSEFFY

Historical and Analytical Comments by
JAMES HUNEKER

G. SCHIRMER, Inc.

DISTRIBUTED BY

7777 W. BLUEMOUND RD. P.O. BOX 13819 MILWAUKEE, WI 53213

THE PRELUDES

I

THE Preludes bear the opus number 28 and are dedicated to J. C. Kessler, a well-known composer of piano studies during Chopin's time. But it is only the German edition that bears his name, the French and English editions being inscribed by Chopin "à son ami Pleyel." As Pleyel advanced the pianist 2,000 francs for these compositions he had the right to say: "These are my Preludes." Niecks is authority for the remark of Chopin: "I sold the Preludes to Pleyel because he liked them." This was in 1838, when Chopin's health demanded a change of climate; he wished to go to Majorca with George Sand and her children, and had applied for money to the piano-maker and publisher, Camille Pleyel of Paris. He received but five hundred francs in advance, the balance being paid on delivery of the manuscript. The Preludes were published in 1839, yet there is internal evidence that proves most of them had been composed before the trip to the Balearic Islands. This fact may upset the pretty legend of music-making at the monastery of Valdemoso. Have we not all read with sweet credulity the eloquent pages by George Sand in which is described the storm that overtook the novelist and her son Maurice! After terrible trials, dangers, delays, they reached home and found Chopin at the piano. Uttering a cry he arose and stared at the storm-beaten pair. "Ah! I knew well that you were dead!" It was the sixth Prelude, the one in B minor, that he played, and dreaming, as Sand writes, "that he saw himself drowned in a lake; heavy, cold drops of water fell at regular intervals on his breast; and when I called attention to those drops of water which were actually falling on the roof, he denied having heard them. He was even vexed at what I translated by the term 'imitative harmony.' He protested with all his might, and he was right, against the puerility of these imitations for the ear. His genius was full of mysterious harmonies of nature."

Yet this Prelude was composed previous to the Majorcan episode. "The Preludes," says Niecks, "consist, to a great extent at least, of pickings from the composer's portfolios, of pieces, sketches and memoranda written at various times and kept to be utilized when occasion might offer." Gutmann, a pupil who nursed Chopin to the end, declared the Preludes to have been composed before he went away with Madame Sand, and to Niecks personally Gutmann maintained that he copied all

of them. Niecks, however, does not altogether credit him, as there are letters in which several of the Preludes are mentioned as being sent to Paris; so he reaches the conclusion that "Chopin's labors at Majorca on the Preludes were confined to selecting, filing and polishing." This seems a sensible solution. Robert Schumann wrote of these Preludes: "I must signalize them as most remarkable. I confess I expected something quite different, carried out in the grand style of his Studies. It is almost the contrary here; these are sketches, the beginning of studies, or, if you will, ruins, eagle's feathers, all strangely intermingled. But in every piece we find in his own hand—'Frédéric Chopin wrote it.' One recognizes him in his pauses, in his impetuous respiration. He is the boldest, the proudest, poet-soul of his time. To be sure, the book also contains some morbid, feverish, repellent traits, but let every one look in it for something that will enchant him. Philistines, however, must keep away."

It was in these Preludes that Ignaz Moscheles first comprehended Chopin and his methods of execution. The German pianist had found his music harsh and dilettantish in modulation, but Chopin's original performance—"he glides lightly over the keys in a fairy-like way with his delicate fingers"—quite reconciled the elder man to this strange music. To Liszt the Preludes are too modestly named, but he dwells too much on Chopin's "marked irritability and exhaustion." Liszt, as usual, erred on the side of sentimentality. Chopin, essentially a man of moods, like many great poets, cannot always be pinned down to any particular period. Several of the Preludes are morbid, as is some of his early music, while just before his death he seems quite gay. "The Preludes follow out no technical idea, are free creations on a small basis and exhibit the musician in all his versatility . . . much is embryonic . . . Often it is as though they were small falling-stars dissolved into tones as they fall." Thus Louis Ehlert. Jean Kleczynski thinks that "people have gone too far in seeking in the Preludes for traces of the misanthropy and weariness of life to which he was a prey during his sojourn in Majorca," and asks if the D minor, the last Prelude of the series, is not strong and energetic, "concluding as it does with three cannon-shots." The truth is, Niecks is right. Mr. Henry James, always an admirer of Madame

Sand, and a friend, admits her utter unreliability; therefore we may consider that her evidence, while romantic, is by no means unimpeachable. So the case stands: Chopin may have written a few of the Preludes at Majorca, filed at them, finished them, but the majority were in his portfolio by 1837 and 1838. Opus 45, a separate Prelude, in C sharp minor, was published December, 1841. It was composed at Nohant, in August of that year, and was dedicated to Mme. la Princesse Elisabeth Czernicheff, whose name, as Chopin confessed in a letter, he did not know how to spell.

II

The first Prelude has all the characteristics of an impromptu. We know the Bach Preludes, which grew out of a free improvisation to be the collection of dance-forms called a Suite, and the Preludes which precede his fugues. In the latter Bach sometimes exhibits the objectivity of the study or toccata, and often wears his heart in full view. Chopin's Preludes—the only preludes to be compared with Bach's—are personal and intimate. This first one is not Bach-ian, yet it could have been written by no one but a devout Bach student. The pulsating, agitated quality of the piece is modern, so is the changeful modulation. It is a composition that rises to no dramatic heights, but is vital and full of questioning. Desperate, and exasperating to the nerves, is the second Prelude in A minor. It is an asymmetrical tune. Chopin seldom wrote ugly music, but is this not, if not exactly ugly, at least despairing, grotesque, even discordant? It suggests in its sluggish, snake-like progression the deepest depression. The tonality is vague, beginning in E minor. Chopin's method of parallelism is clear. A small figure is repeated in descending keys until hopeless gloom and melancholy are attained in the closing chords. Here are all of Chopin's morbid, antipathetic characteristics. Aversion to life, self-induced hypnosis, and emotional atrophy are present. That the Preludes are a sheaf of moods loosely held together by the rather vague title is demonstrated by the third in G. The rippling, rain-like figure assigned to the left hand is in the nature of a study; the melody is delicate, Gallic in spirit. A true salon piece, yet this Prelude escapes artificiality. It is in mood the precise antithesis to the previous one. Gay and graceful, the G major Prelude is a fair reflex of Chopin's sensitive and naturally buoyant nature. It requires a light hand and nimble fingers. The melodic idea calls for no special comment.

Niecks truthfully names the fourth Prelude in E minor "a little poem, the exquisitely sweet, languid pensiveness of which defies description. The composer seems to be absorbed in the narrow sphere of his ego, from which the wide, noisy world is for the time shut out." For Karazowski it is a "real gem, and alone would immortalize the name of Chopin as a poet." It may have been this that impelled Rubinstein to assert that the Preludes were the pearls of the Chopin works. This tiny Prelude contains wonderful music. The grave reiteration of the theme could have suggested to Peter Cornelius his song "Ein Ton." Chopin expands a melodic unit and one singularly pathetic. The whole is like some canvas of Rembrandt— Rembrandt who first dramatized the shadow in which a single motive is powerfully handled; some sombre effect of echoing in the profound of a Dutch interior, all gold and gloom. For background Chopin has substituted his soul; no one in art but Bach or Rembrandt could paint as Chopin did in this composition. Its despair has the antique flavor, and there are breadth, nobility and proud submission quite free from the tortured complaints of the second Prelude. The picture is small, but the subject looms large in meanings. The fifth Prelude in D is Chopin at his happiest. Its arabesque pattern conveys a charming content; and there is a dewy freshness, a joy in life, that puts to flight the morbid tittle-tattle about Chopin's sickly soul. The few bars of this Prelude reveal musicianship of the highest order. The harmonic scheme is intricate; Chopin spinning his finest, his most iridescent web. The next Prelude in B minor is doleful and pessimistic. As George Sand said: "It precipitates the soul into a frightful depression." With the Prelude in D flat it is the most frequently played and often meaninglessly. Classic is its pure contour, its repression of feeling. The echo effect is skillfully managed, monotony artfully avoided. (The duality of the voices should be clearly indicated.) The plaintive, mazurka-like seventh Prelude in A is a mere silhouette of the natural dance; yet in its few measures is compressed all Mazovia. In some editions there is a variant in the fourth bar from the last, a G sharp instead of an F sharp. It is a more piquant climax, perhaps not an admissible one to the Chopin purist. In the F sharp minor Prelude, No. 8, Chopin gives a taste of his best manner. For Niecks the piece is jerky and agitated, and doubtless suggests a mental condition bordering on anxiety; but if frenzy there is, it is kept well in check by the exemplary taste of the composer. The sadness is rather elegiac and less poignant than in the E minor Prelude. On the second page harmonic heights are reached, while the ingenuity of the figure and avoidance of rhythmic monotone are evidences of Chopin's sense of the decorative. It is a masterly Prelude.

There is a measure of grave content in the E major Prelude, the ninth. It is rather gnomic and contains hints of both Beethoven—and Brahms. It has an ethical quality, but that may be suggested by its churchly color and rhythm. The C sharp minor Prelude, No. 10, must be the "ruins and eagle's feathers" of Schumann's criticism. There is a flash of steel-gray, deepening into black, and then the vision vanishes as though some huge bird had plunged down through the blazing sunlight, leaving a color-echo in the void. Or, to be less figurative, this Prelude is a study in arpeggio, with interspersed double-notes, and is too brief to make more than a vivid impression. Number 11, in B, is all too short. It is vivacious, sweet and cleverly constructed. Another gleam of Chopin sunshine. Stormclouds gather in the G sharp minor, the twelfth Prelude, and in its driving *presto* we feel the passionate clench of the composer's hand. He is convulsed with woe, but the intellectual grip, the self-command, are never lost in these two pages of almost perfect writing. The figuration is admirable, and there is a well-defined technical problem. Disputed territory is here; the various editors do not agree about the eleventh and twelfth bars from the last. According to Breitkopf & Härtel, the bass octaves are both times in E. Mikuli gives G sharp the first time, instead of E; Klindworth G sharp the second time, Riemann E, and Kullak the same. In the thirteenth, the F sharp major Prelude, there is atmosphere, pure and peaceful. The composer has found mental rest. Exquisitely poised are his pinions for flight, and in the *più lento* he wheels majestically above in the blue; the return to earth is the signal for some strange modulatory tactics. It is an impressive close.

The fourteenth Prelude, E flat minor, with its heavy, sullen-arched triplets, recalls the last movement of the B flat minor Sonata; but there is less interrogation in this Prelude, less sophistication, and the heat of conflict is over it all. The pulse-beat of the composer increases, and with ill-stifled rage he rushes into battle. There is not a break in the turmoil until the beginning of the fifteenth, the familiar Prelude in the pleasant key of D flat major.

III

This one must be George Sand's: "Some of them create such vivid impressions that the shades of dead monks seem to rise and pass before the hearer in solemn and gloomy funereal pomp." The work needs no programme. Its serene beginning, lugubrious interlude, with the dominant-pedal never ceasing, a *basso ostinato*, lends color to Kleczynski's contention that the sixth Prelude in B minor is a mere sketch of the idea fully elaborated in No. 15. To Niecks, "the C sharp minor portion affects one as if in an oppressive dream: The reëntrance of the opening D flat, which dispels the dreadful nightmare, comes upon one with the smiling freshness of dear, familiar nature." This Prelude wears a nocturnal character. Like the C sharp minor Study in opus 25, it has become slightly banal from repetition; but its beauty, balance and formal chastity there is no disputing. Its architecture is at once Greek and Gothic. The sixteenth Prelude in the relative key of B flat minor is the boldest of the set. Its scale figures—seldom employed by Chopin—boil and glitter, the thematic thread never altogether submerged. Fascinating, full of perilous acclivities and sudden, treacherous descents, this most brilliant of Preludes is Chopin in riotous spirits. He plays with the keyboard. It is an avalanche. Anon a cascade. Then a swift stream, which finally, after mounting to the skies, falls away into an abyss. Full of caprice, imaginative life and stormy dynamics, this Prelude is the darling of the virtuoso. Its pregnant introduction is like a madly jutting rock from which the eagle spirit of the composer precipitates itself. The seventeenth Prelude Niecks finds Mendelssohnian. It is suave, sweet, well-developed, nevertheless Chopin to the core. Its harmonic life is rich and novel. The mood is one of tranquillity. The soul loses itself in autumnal reverie while there is yet splendor on earth and in the skies. Full of tonal contrasts, this highly finished composition is grateful to the touch. The eleven booming A flats on the last page have become celebrated. The fiery recitatives of Prelude No. 18, in F minor, are a glimpse of Chopin, muscular, not hectic. In the various editions you will find three different groupings of the cadenzas. This Prelude is dramatic almost to an operatic degree; sonorous, rather grandiloquent, it is a study in declamation, akin to the declamation of the slow movement in the F minor Concerto. What music is in the nineteenth Prelude in E flat! Its widely dispersed harmonies, its murmuring grace and June-like beauty, are they not the Chopin we best love? He is ever the necromancer, ever evoking phantoms. With its whirring melody and furtive caprice this particular shape is an alluring one. And difficult to interpret with its plangent lyric freedom.

Number 20, in C minor, holds within its bars the sorrow of a nation. Without doubt it is a sketch for a funeral march, and of it George Sand must have been thinking when she wrote that one Prelude of Chopin contains more music than all the trumpetings of Meyerbeer. Of exceeding loveliness is the B flat major Prelude, No. 21. In content and workmanship it is superior to many of the Nocturnes; in feeling and structure it may be said to belong to that form. The melody is enchanting. It arrests one in ecstasy. A period of contemplation sets in and the awakening is almost painful. Chopin, adopting the relative minor key as a pendant to the picture in B flat, thrills the nerves by a bold dissonance in the succeeding Prelude, No. 22. Again, concise paragraphs filled with the smoke of revolt and conflict. The impetuosity of this largely moulded piece in G minor, its daring harmonies—read the seventeenth and eighteenth bars—and sharply-cut dramatic profile make it a worthy companion to the F minor Prelude. Technically considered, it serves as an octave study for the left hand. In the next Prelude, No. 23, in F, Chopin attempted a most audacious feat in harmony (or is it a happy misprint?). An E flat in the bass of the third group of sixteenths leaves the entire composition enigmatically floating in thin air. It deliciously colors the close, evoking a sense of anticipation and suspense; it must have pressed hard on Philistine ears. This Prelude is fashioned from the most volatile stuff. Aerial, imponderable, and like a sun-shot spider-web oscillating in the breeze of summer, its hues change at every puff of air. It is in extended harmonies and must be spiritually interpreted. We have now reached the last Prelude of opus 28. In D minor, it is sonorously tragic, troubled by fevered visions, and capricious, irregular, yet massive in design. It must be placed among Chopin's greater works. The bass requires an unusual span and the thumb of the right hand may eke out the weakness of the left in the case of a small stretch. Like the vast reverberation of monster waves on the implacable coast of a remote world is this Prelude. Despite its fatalistic ring it is not dispiriting. Its issues are more impersonal, more elemental than the other Preludes. It is a veritable *Appassionata*, but its theme is cosmical and no longer behind the closed doors of Chopin's soul. The three tones at the close seem like the final clangor of overthrown reason. After the subjects reappear in C minor there is a shift to D flat; and for a moment a point of repose is achieved; but this rest is elusive. The theme comes back to the tonic and in octaves, and the tension is greater. Then the accumulated passion dissolves in a fierce gust of double chromatic

thirds and octaves and breathless arpeggios. In its pride and scorn this powerful Prelude is at times repellent, but in it I discern no vestige of hysteria. It is as strong, as human, as Beethoven.

The separate Prelude, opus 45, begins with an idea which sounds like Mendelssohn's "Regret" in one of his Songs without Words; but at the thirteenth bar of the Prelude we are landed in the atmosphere of Brahms, the Brahms of the second period, the bitter-sweet lingering, the spiritual reverie in which the music is gently propelled as in a dream. There are the widely extended basses, the shifting harmonic hues, even the bars seem built on Brahmsian lines. Chopin anticipating Brahms is in the nature of a delicate, ironical jest. Of course Brahms owes Chopin little or nothing after his own early E flat minor Scherzo; to Schumann he is more genuinely indebted. The moods of this Prelude are elusive; recondite it is, and not music for the multitude.

Niecks does not think that Chopin created a new type in the Preludes. "They are too unlike each other in form and character," he wrote. Yet, notwithstanding the fleeting, evanescent moods there is a certain unity of feeling and contrasted tonalities, the grouping done in approved Bach-ian order. As if wishing to exhibit his genius in perspective he carved these cameos with exceeding fineness. In a few of them the idea overflows the form; but the majority are exquisite examples of manner and matter, a true blending of voice and vision. Even in the microscopic ones the tracery, like the spirals in exotic sea-shells, is measured. Much in miniature are these sculptured Preludes of the Polish poet.

James Huneker

Thematic Index.
Preludes

PRELUDES

3

À J. C. Kessler

Prélude

Edited and fingered by
Rafael Joseffy

F. Chopin. Op. 28, No. 1

Agitato

1.

Printed in the U.S.A.

23454 x *Copyright, 1915, by G. Schirmer, Inc.*   *Copyright renewed, 1943, by G. Schirmer, Inc.*

Prélude

Edited and fingered by
Rafael Joseffy

F. Chopin. Op. 28, No. 2

2.

Lento

Copyright, 1915, by G. Schirmer, Inc.

Prélude

Edited and fingered by
Rafael Joseffy

F. Chopin. Op. 28, No. 3

*) Carl Tausig, who had a marked preference for a stretchedout position of the fingers, used the following fingering:

Copyright, 1915, by G. Schirmer, Inc.

Prélude

Edited and fingered by
Rafael Joseffy

F. Chopin. Op. 28, No. 4

Largo

4.

Prélude

**Edited and fingered by
Rafael Joseffy**

F. Chopin. Op. 28, No. 5

Allegro molto

25454

Copyright, 1915, by G. Schirmer, Inc.

Prélude

Edited and fingered by
Rafael Joseffy

F. Chopin. Op. 28, No. 6

Lento assai

6.

25454

Prélude

Edited and fingered by
Rafael Joseffy

F. Chopin. Op. 28, No. 7

Andantino

7.

p dolce

Klindworth

Prélude

F. Chopin. Op. 28, No. 8

Molto agitato

8.

p

f

dimin.

*) Various modes of practising:

r.h. a.)

b.) *legato*

etc.

6

6

c.) *6* *6*

etc.

etc.

l.h. a.)

legato

etc.

b.)

etc.

Copyright, 1915, by G. Schirmer, Inc.

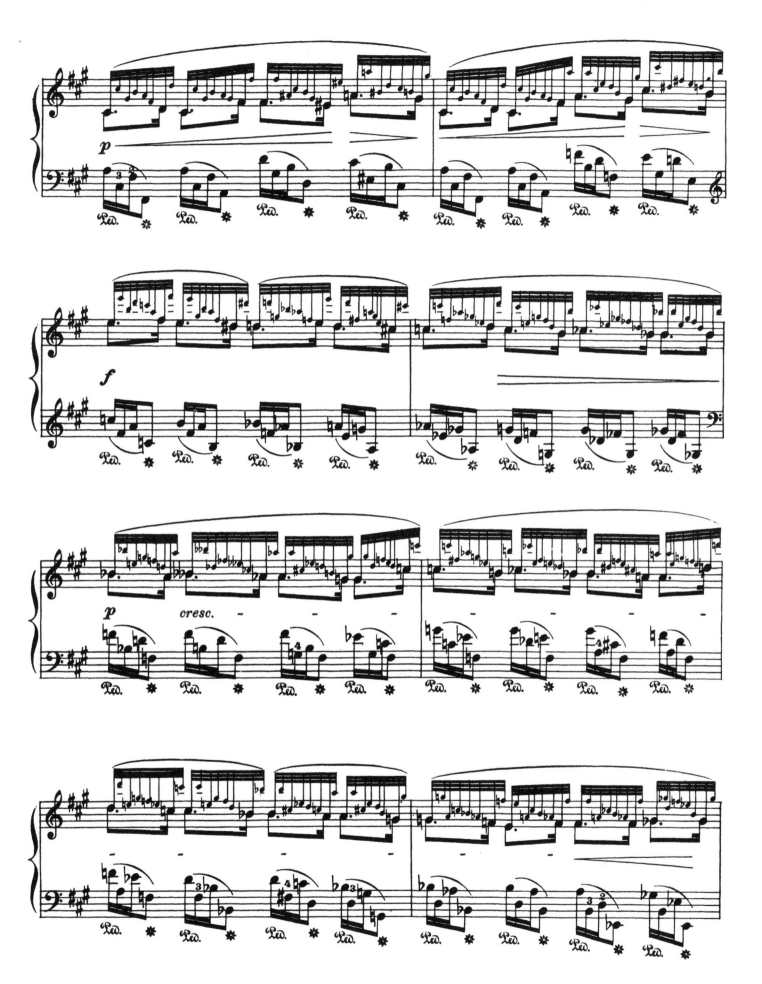

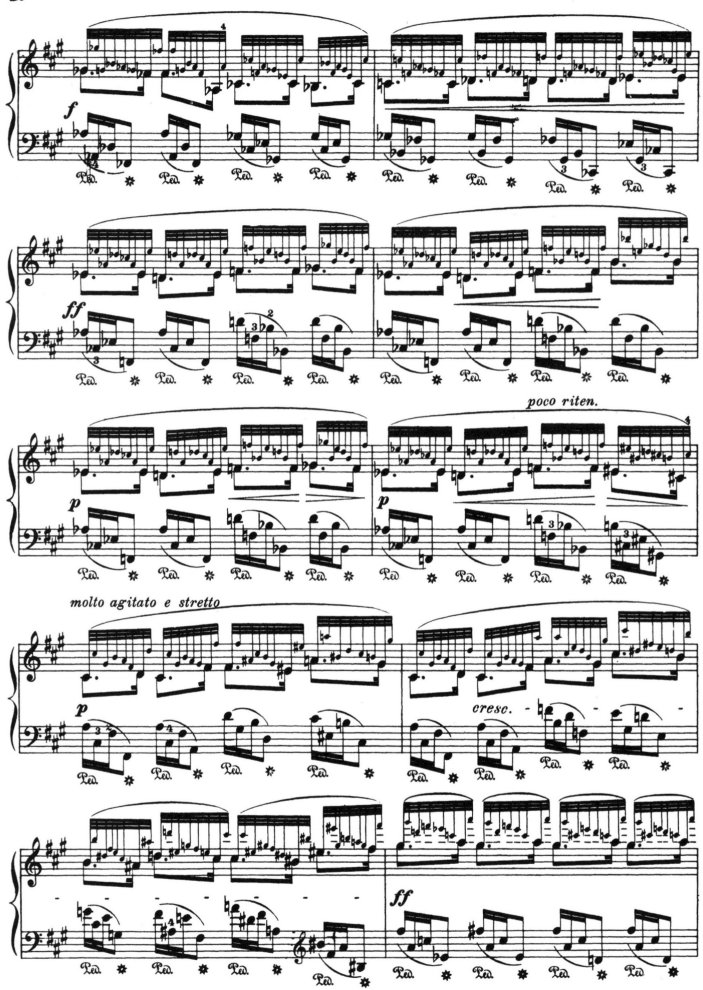

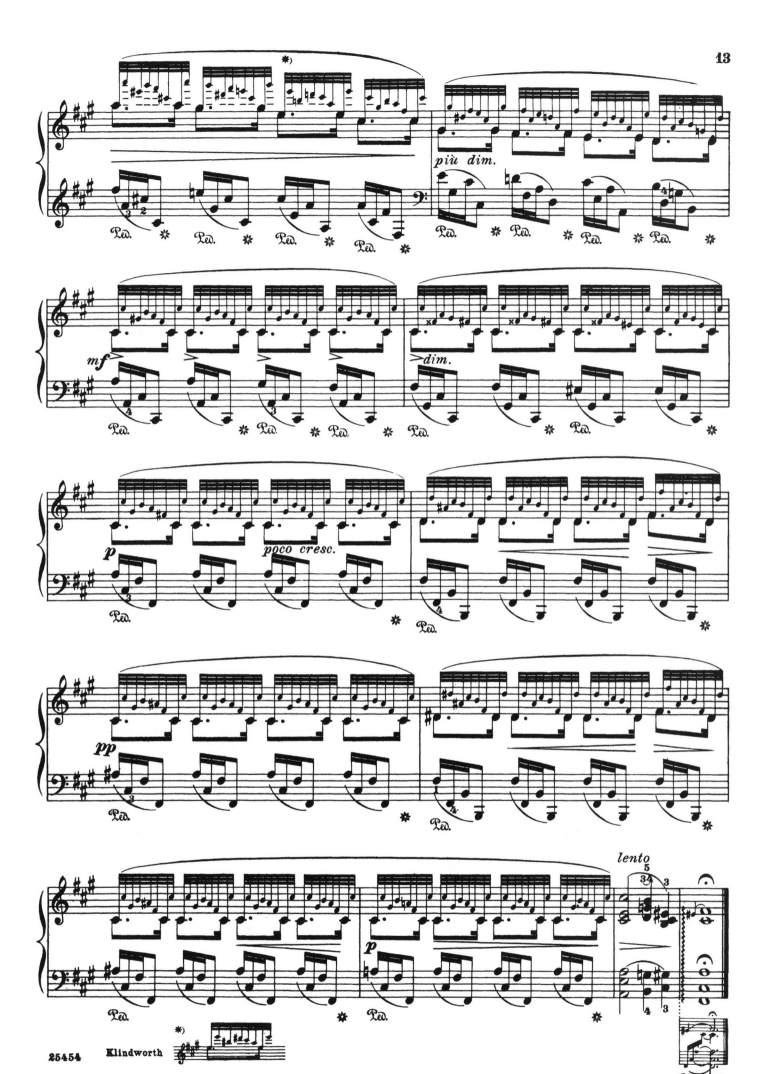

Klindworth

Prélude

Edited and fingered by
Rafael Joseffy

F. Chopin. Op. 28, No. 9

*)Scholz:

Prélude

Edited and fingered by
Rafael Joseffy

Allegro molto

F. Chopin. Op. 28, No. 10

10.

p leggiero

Copyright, 1915, by G. Schirmer, Inc.

Prélude

Edited and fingered by
Rafael Joseffy

F. Chopin. Op. 28, No. 11

25454

Prélude

Edited and fingered by
Rafael Joseffy

F. Chopin. Op. 28, No. 12

Prélude

Edited and fingered by
Rafael Joseffy

F. Chopin. Op. 28. No. 13

Edited and fingered by
Rafael Joseffy

Prélude

Allegro

F. Chopin. Op. 28, No. 14

14.

Prélude

Edited and fingered by
Rafael Joseffy

F. Chopin. Op. 28, No. 15

25454

25454

Prélude

Edited and fingered by
Rafael Joseffy

F. Chopin. Op. 28, No.16

Presto con fuoco

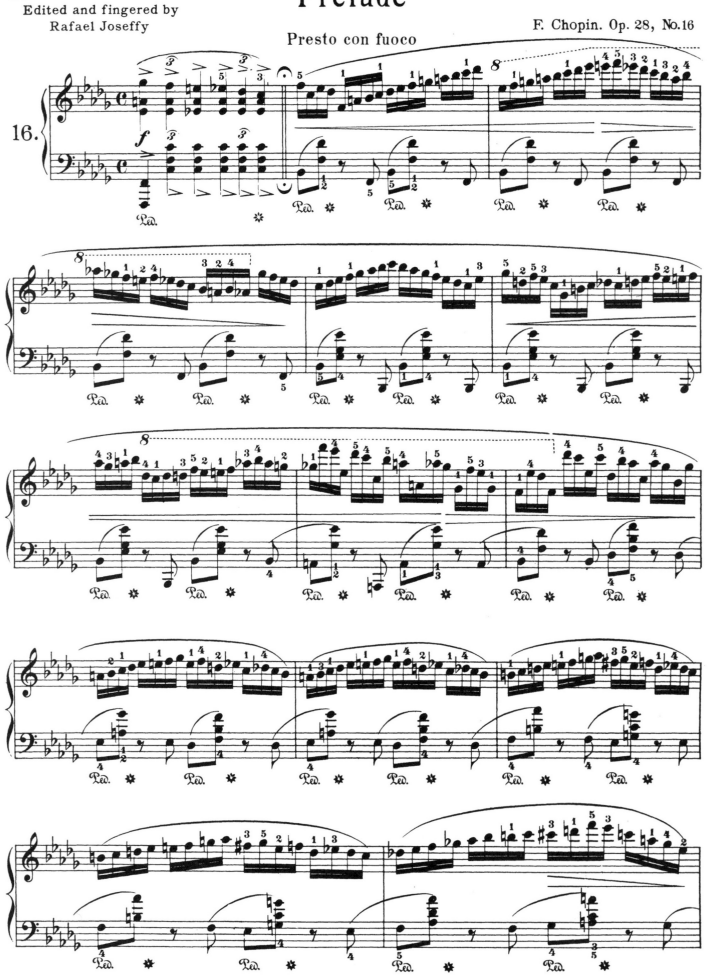

Copyright, 1915, by G. Schirmer, Inc.

25454

Edited and fingered by
Rafael Joseffy

Prélude

F. Chopin. Op. 28, No. 17

Copyright, 1915, by G. Schirmer, Inc.

25454

Prélude

Edited and fingered by
Rafael Joseffy

F. Chopin. Op. 28, No. 18

Klindworth:

Edited and fingered by
Rafael Joseffy

Prélude

F. Chopin. Op. 28, No. 19

Vivace

legato e sempre leggiero

19.

Prélude

Edited and fingered by
Rafael Joseffy

F. Chopin. Op. 28, No. 20

33570

Prélude

F. Chopin. Op. 28, No. 21

25454

Prélude

Edited and fingered by
Rafael Joseffy

F. Chopin. Op. 28, No. 22

Copyright, 1915, by G. Schirmer, Inc.

Prélude

Edited and fingered by
Rafael Joseffy

Moderato

F. Chopin. Op. 28, No. 23

23.

p delicatiss.

Copyright, 1915, by G. Schirmer, Inc.

Prélude

Edited and fingered by
Rafael Joseffy

F. Chopin. Op. 28, No. 24

Allegro appassionato

24.

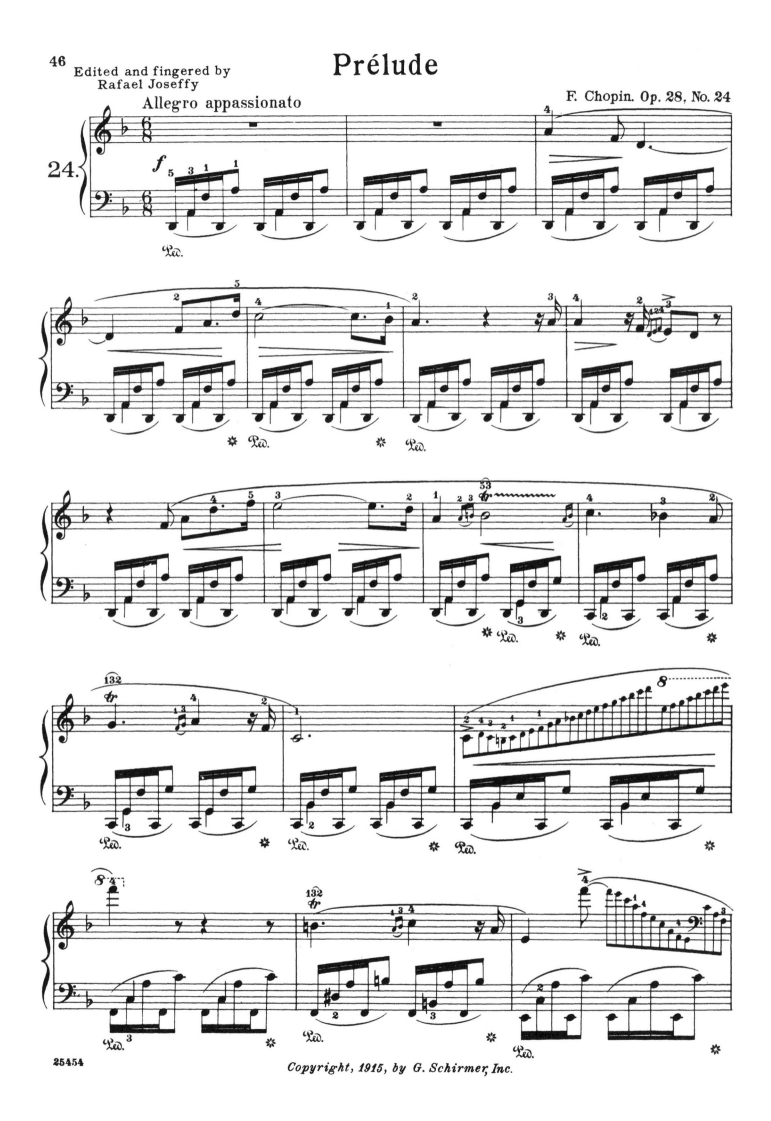

25454

25454

À Mlle la Princesse Élisabeth Czernicheff

Prélude

Edited and fingered by
Rafael Joseffy

F. Chopin. Op. **45**

25.